Extreme Readers

EMERGING
2
READER

Amazing Creations

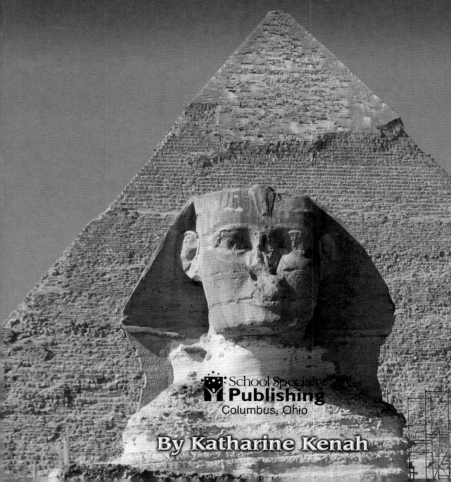

School Specialty
Publishing
Columbus, Ohio

By Katharine Kenah

Copyright © 2007 School Specialty Publishing, a member
of the School Specialty Family.

Printed in the United States of America. All rights reserved. Except as permitted
under the United States Copyright Act, no part of this publication may be
reproduced or distributed in any form or by any means, or stored in a database or
retrieval system, without prior written permission from the publisher, unless
otherwise indicated.

Library of Congress Cataloging-in-Publication Data is on file with the publisher.

Send all inquiries to:
School Specialty Publishing
8720 Orion Place
Columbus, OH 43240-2111

ISBN 0-7696-4336-1

1 2 3 4 5 6 7 8 9 10 PHX 10 09 08 07 06

There are many amazing creations
on earth.
Some of these creations are man–made.
Thousands of people visit these places
every year.
Have you seen any of these
amazing creations?

Stonehenge

Look at what is in England!
Stonehenge is a very old creation.
It is made of huge stones.
The stones form circles.
Some people think that Stonehenge
was a kind of church.

Pyramid and
Great Sphinx

Look at what is in Egypt!
People built this pyramid
over 4,000 years ago.
It is made of thousands of stone blocks.
The blocks are as big and heavy
as trucks.
The Great Sphinx is also very old.
It has the face of a man and the body
of a lion.

Great Wall of China

Look at what is in China!
The Great Wall of China
is the longest creation on earth.
It is about 4,000 miles long.
The wall is so long that it can be seen
from outer space!

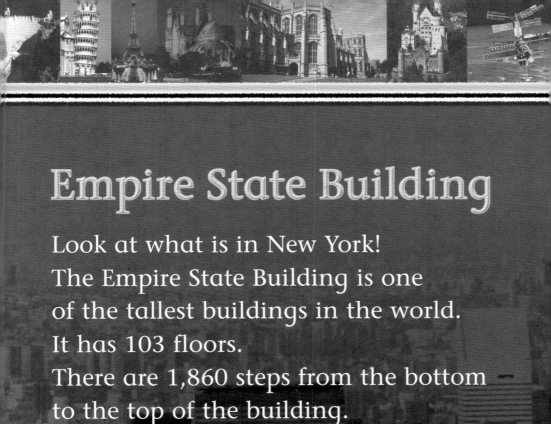

Empire State Building

Look at what is in New York!
The Empire State Building is one
of the tallest buildings in the world.
It has 103 floors.
There are 1,860 steps from the bottom
to the top of the building.

Mount Rushmore

Look at what is in South Dakota!
Mount Rushmore is a sculpture
of four American presidents.
Their faces are cut into the side
of a cliff.
It took over ten years to carve
the faces out of the rock!

Golden Gate Bridge

Look at what is in California!
The Golden Gate Bridge is one
of the largest bridges in the world.
It crosses part of the San Francisco Bay.
The Golden Gate Bridge is not gold.
It is really orange!

The White House

Look at what is in Washington, D.C.!
The White House is the home
of the President of the United States.
It has 132 rooms and 35 bathrooms.
The President works on the first floor.
The President's family lives
on the second floor.

Hoover Dam

Look at what is between Nevada
and Arizona!
The Hoover Dam is a huge, high wall.
It is as tall as a 70-story building.
The Hoover Dam crosses
the Colorado River.
Water flows through the dam
and runs machines that make electricity.

Leaning Tower of Pisa

Look at what is in Italy!
The Tower of Pisa is a bell tower.
It is nearly 1,000 years old.
After the Tower of Pisa was built,
it started to tip over.
That was because the ground under it
was soft.
Scientists found ways to keep it
from falling.

Eiffel Tower

Look at what is in Paris, France!
The Eiffel Tower was built
for the World's Fair in 1889.
It is 986 feet tall.
This is about as tall as 170 people!
The tower is made of iron and steel.

Notre Dame

Look at what else is in Paris, France!
Notre Dame is a large, famous church.
It has three big rose windows.
The windows are made of colored glass
and shaped like roses.
Stone animals, called *gargoyles*,
line the edges of the roof.

Windsor Castle

Look at what is close to London!
Windsor Castle is home
to the kings and queens of England.
The castle covers as much ground
as nine football fields.
When the queen is at home,
a special flag flies above the castle.

Neuschwanstein Castle

Look at what is in Germany!
Neuschwanstein Castle was built
for King Ludwig of Bavaria
over 150 years ago.
The castle had running water, toilets,
heat, and bathtubs.
This castle was the model for the
Sleeping Beauty Castle at Disneyland®!

International Space Station

Look at what is in outer space!
Many astronauts and scientists
work inside the space station.
They live there and study outer space.
The space station goes around the earth
one time every 92 minutes.

EXTREME FACTS ABOUT AMAZING CREATIONS!

- The large stones in the outer ring of Stonehenge weigh about 28 tons, as much as 20 cars!

- Bandits broke off the Great Sphinx's nose over a thousand years ago.

- If the Great Wall of China had been built in a straight line, it would stretch from Chicago to the North Pole.

- The Empire State Building has a lightning rod on top of it. It gets hit by lightning about 100 times a year.

- If a person had a head the size of George Washington's head on Mount Rushmore, his or her body would be 465 feet tall, taller than a football field.

- A safety net hung under the Golden Gate Bridge while it was being built. The net saved the lives of 19 men who worked on the bridge.

- The White House has its own swimming pool, bowling alley, and movie theater.

- The Hoover Dam weighs 6.6 million tons.

- It takes 294 steps to reach the bell tower at the top of the Leaning Tower of Pisa.

- It takes 50 tons of paint to cover the Eiffel Tower. It is painted every seven years.

- There is room for 6,000 people to attend church in Notre Dame at the same time.

- Windsor Castle is the only royal castle that has been lived in since the Middle Ages.

- King Ludwig drowned in a lake before Neuschwanstein Castle was completed. He never got to live in the finished castle.

- The International Space Station has room for three astronauts at one time.